GOAT

HOUSING, BEDDING,

FENCING, EXERCISE YARDS

AND PASTURE

MANAGEMENT GUIDE

Felicity McCullough

Paperback Edition

My Lap Shop Publishers
Plymouth, England
www.mylapshop.com

ISBN: 978-1-78165-041-7

Series: Goat Knowledge 7

Disclaimer

This book is meant to be STRICTLY an Educational and Informational Tool only. The suggestions contained in this material might not be suitable for everyone. It is not intended to provide diagnosis or treatment. The author obtained the information from sources believed to be reliable and from personal experience. Although the best effort was made by the author, there are no guarantees as to the accuracy or completeness of the contents within this work.

The author does not guarantee the accuracy of any information or content in resources or websites listed or cited within this work. Additionally, the author, publisher and distributors never give medical, legal, accounting or any other type of professional advice. The reader must always seek those services from competent professionals that can review the particular circumstances. Mention of any product, brand or website is NOT an endorsement or recommendation of that product, service or usage.

The medical field is a very dynamic field that is constantly undergoing research, modifications and advancements and therefore information contained in this book should always be researched further and A VETERINARIAN OR OTHER SPECIALIST SHOULD BE CONSULTED where appropriate.

Any and all application of the information contained in this book is of the sole responsibility of the person performing said action. The author, publisher and distributors particularly disclaim any liability, loss, or risk taken by individuals who directly or indirectly act on the information herein. All readers must accept full responsibility for their use of this material.

Acknowledgement

The publisher thanks Danielle Shurskis for her support and help in bringing these series of books and articles to publication.

My Lap Shop Publishers

Table of Contents

Introduction

Goats, like all animals, have their own needs in terms of facilities and land. This mini eBook will be focused on what goats need to stay healthy and happy. We will discuss the facilities that you will need in order to keep and raise goats.

Goats require the basic necessities of food, water and shelter. So we will discuss the facilities associated with these things, specifically pasture, fencing, housing and exercise yards.

The specific facilities that you require will depend on your reason for having goats. For instance, if you run a meat goat farm, you may only require a pasture with food and water containers and a crude, three-sided shelter. On the other hand, dairy goat farms might require the goats be confined, with several buildings dedicated to the business.

Fencing

Fencing is very important for confinement and protection against predators. You are looking for a fence that will have the longest life and need the least amount of maintenance. No one wants to be spending all their time fixing fencing.

Considerations

When considering exactly what type of fencing is best for your property, there are a few things you will want to consider.

First, are your goats horned? Horns can be helpful when managing the goat and it is definitely the most natural for the goat. Unfortunately, horns also tend to get the goat stuck in certain types of fences.

If you have horned goats, you will either want a fence where the goat cannot put its head through, which is preferable, or one that has big enough spaces that it can put its head through and back. Permanent electric fencing is an example of one that the goat cannot put its head through.

Another factor to consider is the type of predators in the area. Five-strand high tensile electric fence is very efficient against dogs and coyotes. The major disadvantage with this type of fencing is the need for electricity and to maintain the area around the fencing free of vegetation.

You should also consider the cost of the fencing and how long it will probably last. If you pay a lot of money, it should at least last a long time. Two other factors for consideration are the maintenance required and the effectiveness of containing the livestock.

Try to angle the corners, or use stock panels across existing corners. Goats are herd animals and will occasionally pile up in a corner, leading to injury of animals and damage to fencing.

There are a number of materials that can be used for fencing, each with its own advantages and disadvantages.

Planning

When you are planning on fencing, the best thing to do would be to take a nice, big aerial photo of your property and overlay a sheet of clear plastic. Then you can draw where you want your fencing. You will also need to consider gateways, how you run your farm and how the animals move.

For instance, if you rotate your animals, you will need to consider roadways and how to transport animals. Also consider where you are going to put your energizers and the ground as well as the direction of the electric current.

Types of Fencing

The possible options include barbed wire, cable, woven wire, net wire, and electric fencing. We will discuss the advantages and disadvantages of each option below.

Steel wire is protected by a coating around the wire in a process called galvanization. The type and thickness of this coating is the most important factor when dealing with the longevity of the wire, as well as cost. Generally speaking, there are three classes of galvanization: Class 1, 2 and 3 with 1 having the lightest coating and 3 having the thickest.

Zinc is most commonly used to coat steel wires. The thicker the layer, the more time it will take before the wire rusts. In other words, the more ounces of zinc per square foot of wire surface, the more years it will be before it starts to rust.

The wire must be tied off at the corner post with a strong knot that is self-locking. A simple way to do this is by making sure that the insulator is within eight inches of the post and by wrapping the wire around itself, at least four times. Use a figure eight knot, or reef knot to join wires in the middle of the fence line.

Barbed Wire

Barbed wire fencing is made up of two strands of galvanized wire twisted together. Every four or five inches there are two or four barbs. You can find 12 ½ gauge, 13 ½ gauge or gaucho wire dimensions. The wire is stretched and attached to posts that are evenly spaced from twelve to twenty feet apart.

Barbed wire is one of the most common fencing materials. If used with goats, some adjustments need to be made. For instance, you will need to use five or six wires instead of four or five wires to keep goats in. The bottom spacing should be three inches apart and increase as you go up to about five inches. The total height is normally around 51 to 54 inches. These strands are held apart by twisted wire stays, droppers, or plastic battens.

It is important with this type of fencing that the corner posts are very stable. They need to be able to resist kick out and up-heaving. Barbed wire is easily found and easy to work with, yet can cause injury.

Cable Wire

Cable wire fencing is expensive and less popular these days, being replace by electric fencing. It consists of 3/8 inch steel wire cables stretched between posts with a spring fixed on one end of each cable to absorb shock. Usually six wires are used for large animals and more for smaller animals. The height can vary from 60 to 72 inches.

Woven Wire

Woven wire fencing is made up of smooth wires that form a grid-type pattern. They work very well in containing goats. Normal height used is 39 inches, although this can vary depending on the breed that you are confining. You can find fencing with a height anywhere from 26 inches to 48 inches.

Spacing between wires varies from 1.5 to 9 inches. Stay wires should be spaced from 6 inches or 12 inches apart, depending on the size of the animal. Putting a high tensile electric wire along the bottom will prevent predators from digging under the fence. You can also put the fence flush with the ground and use snares. Be careful with this, because it can lead to rusting.

The advantages of Welded Wire Panels, Cattle Panels and Hog Panels include their easy and quick assembly, rust resistance, as long as contact with soil is avoided and they are available in different heights, dimensions, wire diameters and hole sizes. Unfortunately, sometimes the goats can climb over the fence, or bow it down by leaning on it.

Chain link is easily found at various heights and lengths, rust-free and attractive. The cost rises because it needs posts, top rails, gates and concrete. It may be heavy and difficult to install. Goats can learn to escape by pushing out the bottom.

Mesh Wire

Mesh wire fencing can be found in a diamond pattern or square knot pattern. The square pattern is formed from wires spaced 4 inches apart and stay wires spaced 2 inches apart. Joints are held together with a piece of wire tied into a "knot". The diamond pattern is formed by two wires twisted together and then spaced four inches apart. Stay wires are wrapped in such a way as to form a triangle with a two-inch base.

There are different wire thicknesses available as well, being 11, 12.5, 14 and 16 gauges. Height can vary from 50 to 72 inches. These are typically more expensive fencing options.

Net wire is sold in rolls of 330 feet. You can find this type of fencing in various heights and opening sizes. You can find 48 or 72 inch high woven horse mesh with two by four inch openings in 100, or 200 foot rolls. Another possibility is a 50 or 58 inch high V-mesh that is sold in 165 foot rolls.

This type of fencing is good for land that isn't flat and is readily available. Goats can get their heads caught, though. Also, this type of fencing normally requires two people to build.

Wood Fencing

Board fencing is made of one inch or two inch thick and four to six-inch wide boards nailed to flat posts. Height can vary from 4.5 to 5 feet. You can use lumber, plywood and posts. This type of fencing requires only basic tools for construction and can be built to any type of terrain. The wood can be treated or untreated, painted or unpainted.

Spacing of the posts depends on the length of the boards. Attach the posts on the side of the livestock, so they can't lean against them and push them out.

These fences are expensive to build and maintain, after all wood can rot or break. Maintenance and labour are more costly as well. Care must be taken, because goats will chew and eat the wood, toxins and all, yet if you do not treat or paint the wood, it will eventually rot.

High Tensile Fencing

High Tensile Fencing is easy to install, low maintenance and relatively inexpensive. Eventually it will sag a bit. It can be electrified. Wire used is either eleven or fourteen-gauge wire, with a tensile strength of 170,000 to 200,000 pounds per square inch (psi) and a breaking strength of 1,800 pounds.

Posts are spaced 16 to 90 feet apart. The tension is set using a permanent in-line strainer at 200 to 250 pounds of tension placed in the middle of the wire. You will also need one tension indicator spring on one wire per fence.

Electric Fencing

The animals need to be trained to stay away from electric fencing. The most important aspect in regards to training is making sure that they can see the wire. Often, this means using colours other than black, such as white or orange.

Electric Fencing can be temporary or permanent. A variety of materials can be used for temporary fencing, including the popular Poly Tape. Poly Tape is aluminium, or stainless steel woven with polyethylene fibres that comes in black, orange and white colours. Black is the hardest to see. You can only run Poly tape for about 1,200 feet.

Temporary fencing is used to protect trees and gardens from animals as well as to create temporary paddocks, pens or pastures. Strip grazing is also made possible, which is where a pasture is divided into paddocks. It permits better pasture management.

For permanent fencing, usually smooth wire is used with as many as 10 to 12 strands. Possible materials to use include aluminium, stainless steel, and high tensile wire. Usually every other wire is electrified with the alternate wires serving as grounds.

Permanent electric wire can be run further than temporary electric fencing. This type of wiring is harder to see, which means that it may be more difficult to train the animals to stay away. The problem can be solved by using bright coloured cloth or plastic on the wire, to make it more readily visible.

Run the wires underground at gates. Bury the line at least 12 inches deep and run it through irrigation tubing.

An electric fence requires the wire that is to be electrified, a controller, posts, lead outs, and lightning protection. You may need to construct a flood gate as well, depending on if you have areas of land that periodically flood on your property.

Controller/Charger/Energizer

The fence is electrified with a controller. Other names for this controller are a charger or energizer. The controller is what controls the short bursts of high voltage electricity that is sent out along the wires. The controller can be powered by batteries, solar energy or electricity.

Electric fencing can also be used on old fencing to keep animals from leaning over it, or into it, by using off setting on top of or two thirds down the fence. Usually an offset wire is used either on the top or about two thirds of the way up.

Advantages of electric fencing include the ease of installation, if done properly. Animals, both the goats and predators learn to respect electric fencing. Disadvantages include the ease that the electricity can be disrupted by vegetation, lightning and other things.

Controllers are often given a rating. In essence, though, the rating of fences is just a general comparison, due to the fact that there are no real standards. Each company can measure their fences under different conditions; for instance, at the energizer, or on the fence line and at different loads. On top of this, factors such as soil fertility, soil moisture, length of the fence wire and gauge and vegetation present along the fence line, all will alter the performance of the electric fencing.

Posts

You can use wood, fibre glass, plastic, steel or low-conductivity composites for posts. Wood and steel posts will need insulators. Plastic needs to be treated with ultraviolet inhibitors to prevent fast deterioration in sunlight.

Lead Outs

You should use a 12½ gauge double insulated cable for the lead out. Insulation helps to protect from short-outs. Alternatively, you can use 10- or 8-gauge wires as well. If you combine two or more lead out wires, it is even better in terms of resistance of the wire.

Lead out wires can either be run overhead or underground. If you choose to run it underground, putting them through irrigation tubing is a good idea for extra protection.

Flood Gates

Flood gates are used in areas that periodically flood such as streams. First, string a wire over the stream, connecting to posts on either side. Then you hang galvanized chain every six to twelve inches until about a foot above the lowest water level. The flood gate controller is then connected to both the fence and flood gate.

Lightning

The charger needs to be protected from lightning strike,

which can come from either the input or the output side. The input side is where the electricity comes from and the output side is the fence.

You can use a power surge protector or a fused plug to protect the input side of the charger, which is less commonly hit by lightning. A lightning diverter and choke coil is used for the output side.

Housing and Bedding

Shelter is necessary to protect goats from rain, wind, and cold. Goats are infamous for not liking the rain. What type of housing you choose depends on the size of the herd, the available land and what type of operation you have.

Considerations

When planning shelters, first you must consider your herd size, both current and future, and the land that you have available for use as well as why you are raising goats and your future plans.

Types of Housing

There are a number of types of shelter that you can build for your goats. The different options differ greatly in price, maintenance requirements and types of materials. You can either build from scratch, or modify a pre-existing building, such as calf hutches, or chicken houses.

Bedding used is normally straw, although low-quality hay, wood shavings, and sawdust are other options. In the winter, sometimes new bedding is added on top of old bedding containing manure.

The lower layer of bedding will begin to decompose, creating heat. It is important in the winter that the layer of bedding is nice and thick.

Open Housing

Open housing is basically a roof with at least one wall. You can close in three sides and even all four sides. This is the easiest and least expensive housing option. You need to build this shelter protecting the goats from the prevailing winds.

The roof usually slopes towards the back of the shelter with the front being around five to six feet high and the back from three to four feet high. The length and depth of the shelter varies depending on the number of goats you have with roughly ten to fifteen square feet of bedding per animal.

The shelter can be lined with a bedding of straw or other type or can be plain dirt. You can use treated wood posts, lumber, corrugated sheet iron, welded pipe frames, heavy sheet metal, plywood or other materials to make the frame of the structure. It can be painted, although you should look carefully at the paint to make sure that there are no toxic chemicals, because goats love to chew on the wood.

Confinement Housing

When you want to keep goats in a shelter at all times, this is called confinement. This type of shelter should also have an exercise yard attached to it, which will be discussed below.

Floors

The floor in this type of shelter can be dirt, wood or concrete. Provide at least 20 square feet of space for each goat, not counting the space where the feed and water troughs go.

You should cover the floor with bedding in the winter. Bedding height depends on the flooring material. Dirt floors need around three to four inches, concrete requires around five to six inches and drainage of urine and manure removal.

Lighting

Make sure that you include windows and artificial lighting. There should be around one to two square feet of windows per animal. Sunlight is important for animal health as well as help keeping the shelter disinfected.

Ventilation

Goats need plenty of ventilation and air flow without draughts. If they do not receive proper ventilation, or are exposed to draughts, they will develop respiratory problems.

Fans should be available to pull air down from the ceiling in the summer. Fan capacity should be to move fifteen to two hundred cubic feet of air per minute.

Walls

The walls can be insulated to prevent condensation, which can cause health problems. If you do use insulation, you will need to use plywood, or something similar to cover it, or the goats will eat it all.

Kidding Pens

Kidding pens are convenient and useful. They provide protection from predators and make it easier for the producer to keep an eye for kidding problems. They can be made from pipe and wire panels, wire panels, lumber, chain link fencing, or pretty much anything you can think of and connected together with wire, hog tings or even duct tape.

Dimensions should be around 48 inches high and a minimum of five feet long and five feet wide or six feet long and four feet wide. It should have a nice layer of bedding to keep the kids warm. Usually kids and moms only stay from one to three days in these pens.

Exercise Yards

Goats require exercise for optimum health. An exercise pen is perfect for keeping them in shape. Some people exercise goats by chasing them in the pen or having a muzzled dog put them to run, although this causes undue stress on the animal. You can also lead or walk the goats at a fast pace. This is used most often for show goats.

The exercise pen should have sand or clean soil on the floor and be fenced in with good fencing. Avoid electric fencing for this area. It is best if the walls are solid and curved, so that the goat can only see forward and won't hurt itself on the fencing.

Goat herds usually get enough exercise on their own, especially if maintained in pastures. Pet goats only require a nice, outdoor area equipped with large rocks, large tree branches, or stumps and wooden spools to climb on. They will also play among themselves. Putting the feed trough at one end of a pen and the water at the other also helps to ensure at least a little exercise.

Pastures

Pastures should contain a variety of species such as Blackberries, Willows, Russian Olive, Ryegrass and Multiflora Roses, just to name a few. Wheat, rye and oats are cool season plants. Orchardgrass and Berseem clover with wheat are perennials. Crabgrass, Sudangrass, millet, Johnsongrass and cowpeas grow best in the summer.

Care of pastures is very complex and a large area to cover, too large for this publication. We will be able to only touch on the important subjects.

Managing pastures is done in order to obtain the highest quality plants throughout lactation and to provide forage for as much of the year as possible.

The more time goats are in pasture, the more money is saved by the producer, both in feed and labour, because less time is spent feeding the animals. Even when dairy goats are on pasture, they should be supplemented with grain in order to maximize milk production.

Parasite Control through Pasture Management

You do not want to let the goats overgraze, because if the goats eat plants that are too close to the ground, they will be exposed to more parasites and the plants' ability to regenerate will be compromised. Goats should be moved to another pasture when the plants are roughly three to four inches high.

Another technique that works to manage parasites is to put cows into the pasture after the goats, or you can try tilling or making hay. This works well because most gastrointestinal parasites are species-specific, meaning that those that infect cows will not infect goats. The only exception to this rule is that certain parasites and cross infect goats and sheep.

Annual Soil Testing

Annual soil testing is a good idea both to determine stocking rates as well as for correction to optimize plant growth. Testing will determine the actual need for fertilizer and lime application.

Fifteen to twenty samples from different areas of the pasture need to be collected for a soil test. The samples should be at least six inches deep. The levels of Potassium, Nitrogen and Phosphorus as well as soil pH are especially important to know.

Rotational Grazing

Rotational grazing as well as the annual soil testing enables a producer to have a good pasture, even in years of drought. When properly used, it can also help limit the population of worms, especially when combined with the use of deworming medications.

Group the animals appropriately. Keep dry does, doelings and mature does in separate groups. You may want to combine species or, another option is to move species one after another.

This is a wonderful technique to use because species eat plants differently. For instance, cows eat longer grasses while goats are browsers, preferring brush and other plants that are often considered weeds, such as Willow, Pigweed, Thistles, Stinging Nettle, and Curly Dock.

Plant Types

A mixture of browse and grass is excellent for goats. Two acres of browse to one acre of grassland is a good proportion, according to Darrell Rankins Jr., an

Extension Animal Scientist (Rankins, 2008).

Goats can be fed completely on forage during the summer months, all they need supplemented with are salt and minerals, especially phosphorus.

There are many plant species that can be used for forage, including: Ryegrass, Rye, Wheat, Oats, Bahiagrass, Pearl Millet, Bluegrass, Bermudagrass, Alfalfa, White clover, Orchardgrass, Red clover, Fescue, and Dwarf pearl millet.

These are only a few of the species that are used.

When deciding what to plant in your pasture, you will need to research each plant species to know what their nutritional value is, when they grow, stocking rates and for how long and what the plant needs to grow.

You should plant a nice variety of both warm season and cool season plants, to ensure forage as much of the year as possible. Depending on where you are located, some producers will be forced to supplement with hay during the winter months, when pastures are unavailable due to snow coverage.

Make sure to have good feeders, both for grains as well as hay, if supplementing in pasture. Goats are notorious for wasting food. They will throw hay onto the floor and trample on it. They are also picky eaters, meaning that if hay or grain has been stepped on, they will not eat it.

Resources

Freking, Brian and Kevin Nickols. Chapter 3: Fencing. Oklahoma State University. Available at: - http://meatgoat.okstate.edu/oklah oma-basic-meat-goat-manual-1/Chapter%203%20-%20Fencing.pdf

Orrell, Kent. Meat Goats: 4-H Livestock projects. Oklahoma State University. January 2005. Available at: - http://oces.okstate.edu/kiowa/4-h/Meat%20Goats.pdf.

Rankins, Darrel Jr. Feeding the
Goat Herd. 2008. Alabama
Cooperative Extension System.
Available at: -
http://www.aces.edu/extcomm/ex
tlivestock/LivestockLinksFall08.p
df.

Smith, Tom. Chapter 4: Housing.
Oklahoma State University.
Available at: -
http://meatgoat.okstate.edu/oklah
oma-basic-meat-goat-manual-
1/Chapter%204%20-
%20Housing.pdf

Spencer, Robert. Pasture Management – Goat Style. Alabama Cooperative Extension System, 2008. Available at: - http://www.aces.edu/extcomm/ex tlivestock/LivestockLinksFall08.p df.

My Lap Shop Publishers, 91
Mayflower Street, Unit 222,
Plymouth, Devon PL1 1SB UK

Published By

My Lap Shop Publishers

91 Mayflower Street, Unit 222,

Plymouth, Devon, PL1 1SB

United Kingdom

Tel: +44 (0)871 560 5297

www.mylapshop.com

www.goatlapshop.com

About My Lap Shop Publishers
First Edition September 2012
ISBN - 978-1-78165-040-0

About Felicity McCullough

Felicity McCullough has written several books about preventative health care for goats.

The website dedicated to goats www.goatlapshop.com has a wide variety of topics and resources that relate to goats, including the Charlie And Isabella's Magical Adventures Series of Children's Books, suitable for bed-time reading that are beautifully illustrated.

Goat Knowledge Series Titles

www.goatlapshop.com
www.mylapshop.com

How To Keep Goats Healthy #1
ISBN: 978-1-78165-021-9

Golden Guernsey Goats #2
ISBN: 978-1-78165-022-6

A Simple Guide To The Goat's
Digestive System #3
ISBN: 978-1-78165-024-0

Success Guide For Raising
Healthy Goats #4
ISBN: 978-1-78165-026-4

Managing Goat Nutrition: What
You Need To Know A Simple
Guide #5
ISBN: 978-1-78165-027-1

Plants And Goats An Easy To Read Guide #6

ISBN: 978-1-78165-041-7

Other Goat Books and Articles

by

Felicity McCullough

www.goatlapshop.com
Boar Goats
Charlie And Isabella's Magical Adventure
Charlie And Isabella Meet Jacob
Charlie And Isabella's Second Adventure With Jacob
Charlie And Isabella's Magical Adventures Compendium
Diseases of Goats
Goat Basics
Goat Breed: Golden Guernsey Goats
Goat Videos
How To Keep Goats Healthy
Nigerian Dwarf Goats
Nimbkar Boer Goat
Raising Goats Easy Guide To Raising and Caring for Goats
The Fun of Goats

My Lap Shop Publishers

Plymouth, England

www.mylapshop.com

www.ingramcontent.com/pod-product-compliance
Lightning Source LLC
Chambersburg PA
CBHW070931270326
41927CB00011B/2807